better together*

*This book is best read together, grownup and kid.

a kids
book
about

a kids book about

food

by Asma Khan

A Kids Co.
Editor Emma Wolf
Designer Rick DeLucco
Head of Design Rick DeLucco
CEO and Founder Jelani Memory

DK
Senior Production Editor Jennifer Murray
Senior Production Controller Louise Minihane
Managing Editor Hazel Eriksson
Publishing Director Mark Searle

First published in Great Britain in 2025 by
Dorling Kindersley Limited
20 Vauxhall Bridge Road,
London SW1V 2SA
A Penguin Random House Company

The authorised representative in the EEA is
Dorling Kindersley Verlag GmbH. Arnulfstr. 124, 80636 Munich, Germany

A CIP catalogue record for this book is available from the British Library.

ISBN: 978-0-2417-7660-5

Printed and bound in China

www.dk.com

akidsco.com

MIX
Paper | Supporting
responsible forestry
FSC™ C018179

This book was made with Forest Stewardship Council™ certified paper – one small step in DK's commitment to a sustainable future. Learn more at **www.dk.com/uk/ information/sustainability**

For my sons, Ariz and Fariz, who will
one day become the storytellers
of their culinary heritage.

Intro
for grownups

Food is more than just something we eat. It is a part of us – woven into our history, our families, and our stories. Before you were even born, the smells of your home's cooking surrounded you, whispering the secrets of where you come from.

But sometimes, food can feel like a secret world – one that not everyone understands. Maybe you've worried that someone will say your food smells strange or looks different. Maybe you've wanted to hide it, just to fit in. I understand that feeling.

When I moved far from my homeland, food became my way back. Cooking the dishes of my ancestors reminded me that I belonged. No matter where I was, their flavours connected me to my past.

Your food is a part of you. It tells your story. And when you're ready, you can share that story with the world.

The power and strength of food is hard to

explain in words.

But since this is a book,
I will do my best.

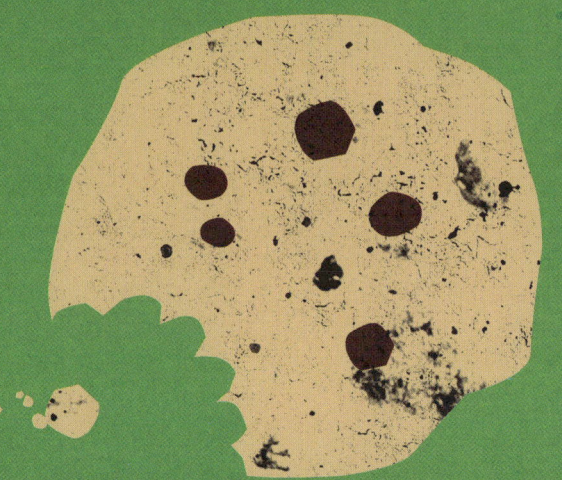

Food
isn't simply
something
you eat.

It's our **DNA** – the very thing we're made of.

It's our **skin tone**, our **accent**, our **culture**, our **history**.

The story of your food has been a part of who you are from before you were even born.

The food you eat
isn't just something
you ask for or pull
from the refrigerator.

...style
...cooked
meat curry in
a thick clingy

Food is given to you,

**passed down,
from generation
to generation.**

Bihari Phulki:
Masoor dal
fritters with
chopped
onions, chillies
and coriander
served with
tamarind
and green

...mpkin Niramishi:
...sonal vegetables
...sed with panch
...ran, a
...itional five-

Maybe it's your great-grandmother's recipe that was passed down to your parents, that you eat every Friday, because that's how it's always been.

Our food is always connected to our families.

Our ancestors.
Our cultures.
Our homelands.

Even before you you could **smell** the

It was present every

In Arabic, we have a word, "**nafs** (نَفْس)".

It means your sense of **self** and **soul**.

Your **nafs** is so close to who you are.

That's where your food exists!
So very close that sometimes you may forget to notice or pay attention to it.

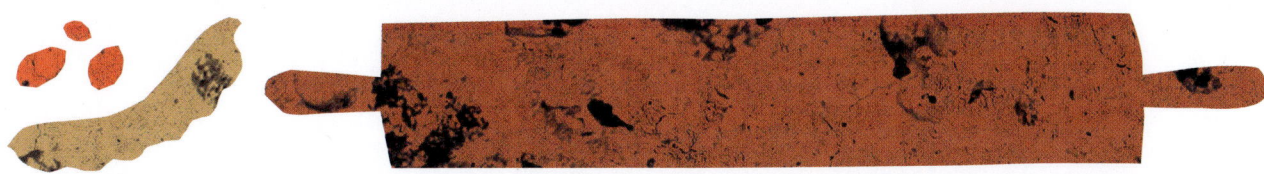

I believe food is kind of like

a secret, hidden world.

Those specific aromas, spices, and experiences.

Other people may not be able to pronounce the words,

but that doesn't make them any less amazing or delicious.

There can be a fear that someone might tell you your food stinks or looks bad.

It can make to talk about

you ashamed
what you eat.

But these smells,
these dishes, they are...

your super, secret power.

Your world
of food is
unique

to you.

And when you want to,
and only when **you** want to,
you can share it with someone else.

These dishes, spices, moments, and flavours are a part of...

♥ who you are.

Those roots extend from where you stand, all the way back to where your history is from.

But this feeling of pride can be difficult to hold onto.

When my older son was growing up, he didn't want to take my food with him to school.

He asked for plain sandwiches and cereal bars – things that would help him "**fit in**".

I knew he didn't like these foods, but he asked for them anyway.

I didn't learn until much later
that he was bullied by other kids
for the foods he brought to school.

Kids would tell him he smelled, and so did his food.

 **At first, I felt** angry at those kids,

 **and then** angry at myself,

 **and then** I just felt sad.

Because my son didn't feel safe to bring a part of himself to school.

He didn't feel like he fit in, **no matter how he tried.**

I want you to know

that it's **OK** to be who you are.

Whatever your
culture, **history**, or **food**...

know that it's special!

Not everyone
will understand it,
or even like it.

But for those special few,
you can invite them into
that secret society.

The smoky infusion of paprika.

The warm
sweetness of
cinnamon.

The earthy
nuttiness of
cumin.

Those flavours are a
part of my secret society,
and you might have your own.

Whatever they may be,
they are a part of your world.

And
that world,
that food,
helps make you
who you are.

Be that person. Don't fear it. Embrace it.

And remember that as simple as it may seem, food is your connection to all of it.

**Like a kiss of spring,
it comes to you.**

It comes from your garden,
to your stove,
and then to your table.

And like a bright medal of honour on your chest it says...

belong.

Outro
for grownups

Food is more than a meal – it is a language of love. A silent way of saying, I care for you, I remember you, I celebrate you. Every dish carries an accent, a rhythm, a melody passed down through time.

The flavours on your plate are stories – stirred with history, myths, and magic. Some recipes are whispered secrets, some are bold declarations, and some are quiet comforts that remind you of home.

Your food tells a story only you can tell. It holds the laughter of your ancestors, the wisdom of your culture, and the warmth of belonging.

So, when you cook, when you eat, when you share a dish with someone special, remember: you are speaking the oldest, most delicious language in the world. And in that language, in every bite, you are saying – you belong.

About The Author

Asma (she/her) moved to Cambridge from Calcutta in 1991. Uprooted and deeply homesick, she began cooking to soothe the emptiness in her soul — and discovered her true calling. She went on to open a restaurant, Darjeeling Express, where she serves the food of her childhood and heritage.

Asma became a storyteller, a cook, a writer, a mother, and an activist for food justice and equality. She believes food has the power to bring people together, and her kitchen is run by an all-female team, giving women opportunities to shine.

Her cookbooks share the flavours and memories of India, and she was the first British chef featured on Netflix's *Chef's Table*. Asma also works with the UN World Food Programme, fighting hunger around the world. Through food, she tells stories of love, history, and hope — always reminding us that a shared meal can change lives.

 @asmakhanlondon

Made to empower.

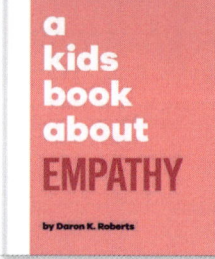
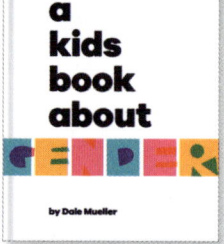

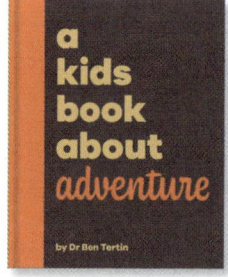
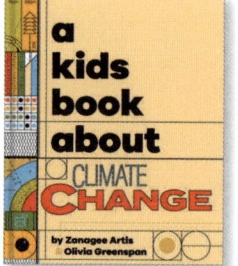

Discover more at akidsco.com